STRUM IT GUITAR

More FAVORITE Songs with 3 CHORDS

T0041101

ISBN 978-0-634-04993-4

HAL•LEONARD® CORPORATION

7777 W. BLUEMOUND RD. P.O. BOX 13819 MILWAUKEE, WI 53213

Visit Hal Leonard Online at
www.halleonard.com

This Publication not for sale in the E.U.

CONTENTS

All Apologies

Words and Music by Kurt Cobain

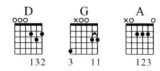

D   G   A

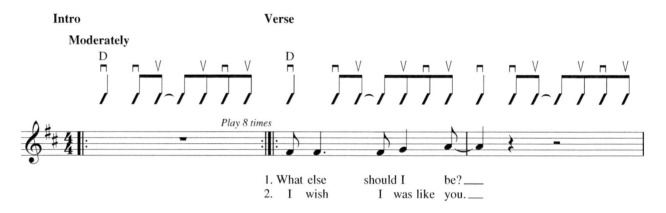

Drop D tuning, down 1/2 step:
(low to high) Db-Ab-Db-Gb-Bb-Eb

Intro　　　　　　　　　　　**Verse**

Moderately

Play 8 times

1. What else should I be? ___
2. I wish I was like you. ___

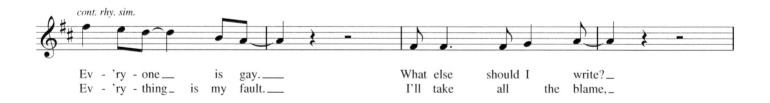

All a-pol - o-gies. ___　　　　What else should I say? ___
eas-i-ly ___ a-mused. ___　　　Find my nest of salt. ___

cont. rhy. sim.

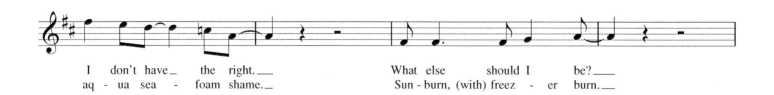

Ev-'ry-one ___ is gay. ___　　　What else should I write? ___
Ev-'ry-thing ___ is my fault. ___　　I'll take all the blame, ___

I don't have ___ the right. ___　　What else should I be? ___
aq-ua sea - foam shame. ___　　Sun-burn, (with) freez - er burn. ___

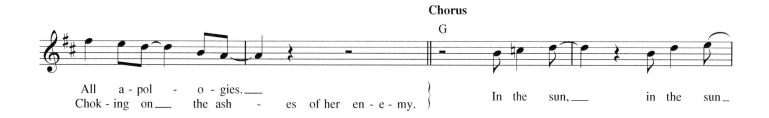

Chorus

G

All a-pol - o - gies.___
Chok - ing on___ the ash - es of her en - e - my.

In the sun,___ in the sun___

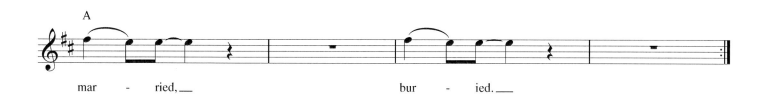

___ I feel___ as one.___ In the sun,___ in the sun...___ (I'm)

A

mar - ried,___ bur - ied.___

Mar - ried,___ bur - ied,___ yeah, yeah,___ yeah, yeah.___

Outro

D   D

___ All a - lone___ is all___

Repeat and fade

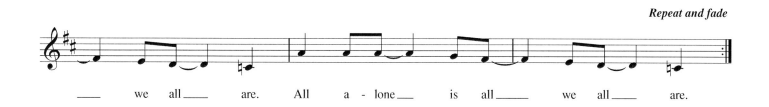

___ we all___ are. All a - lone___ is all_____ we all___ are.

Barbara Ann

Words and Music by Fred Fassert

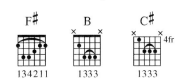

Chorus
Moderately fast

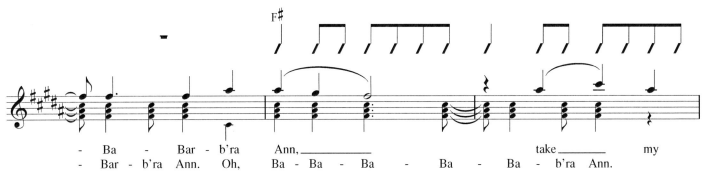

Oh, Ba - Ba - Ba - Ba - Bar - b'ra Ann.   Ba - Ba - Ba - Ba -
(Ba - Ba - Ba - Ba -

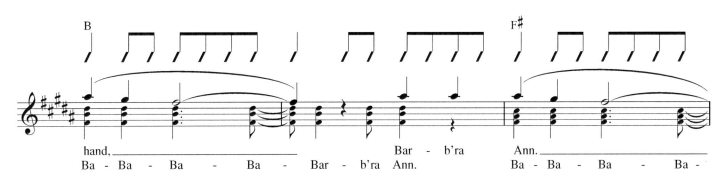

- Ba - Bar - b'ra   Ann, _____ take _____ my
- Bar - b'ra Ann. Oh, Ba - Ba - Ba - Ba - Ba - b'ra Ann.

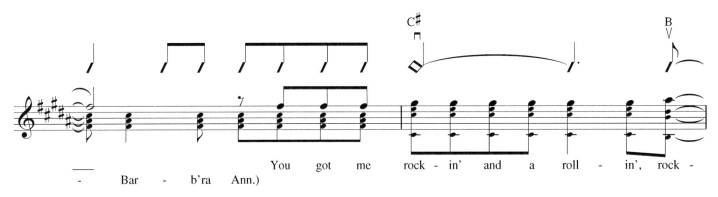

hand, _____ Bar - b'ra   Ann. _____
Ba - Ba - Ba - Ba - Bar - b'ra Ann.   Ba - Ba - Ba - Ba -

You got me rock - in' and a roll - in', rock -
- Bar - b'ra Ann.)

- in' and a reel - in', Bar-b'ra Ann, Ba - Ba - Ba - Bar-b'ra Ann.

7

Chorus

Ba - Ba - Ba - Ba - Bar - b'ra Ann. Ba - Ba - Ba - Ba - Ba - Bar - b'ra
(Ba - Ba - Ba - Ba - Bar - b'ra Ann. Oh,

Ann, _____ take _____ my hand, _____ Ba - Ba - Ba - Ba -
Ba - Ba - Ba - Ba - Ba - b'ra Ann. Ba - Ba - Ba - Ba -

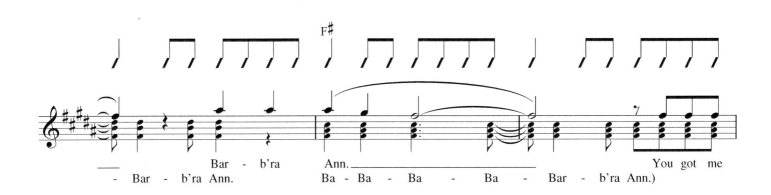

_____ Bar - b'ra Ann. _____ You got me
- Bar - b'ra Ann. Ba - Ba - Ba - Ba - Bar - b'ra Ann.)

To Coda

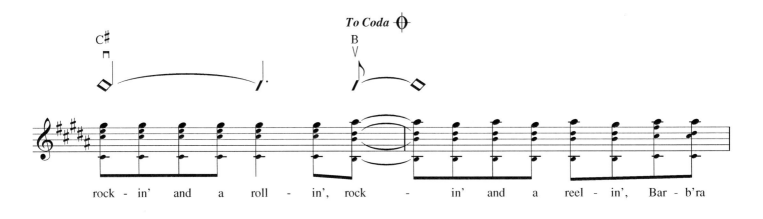

rock - in' and a roll - in', rock - in' and a reel - in', Bar - b'ra

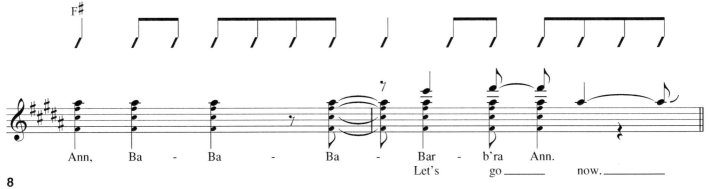

Ann, Ba - Ba - Ba - Bar - b'ra Ann.
Let's go _____ now. _____

Be-Bop-a-Lula

Words and Music by Tex Davis and Gene Vincent

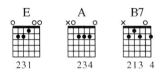

Chorus

Moderately (♩♩ = ♩♪)

Well,_ Be - Bop-a-Lu - la, she's my_ ba - by. Be-Bop-a-Lu - la, I

don't_ mean_ may - be. Be-Bop-a-Lu - la, she's my ba - by. Be-Bop-a-Lu - la, I

don't_ mean_ may - be. Be-Bop-a-Lu - la, she - e - 's___ my ba - by

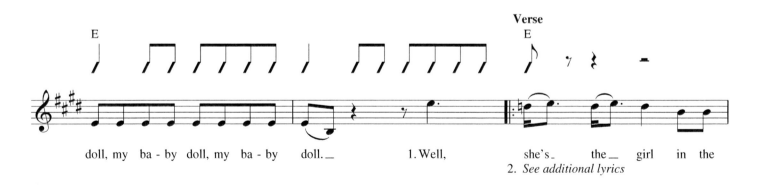

doll, my ba - by doll, my ba - by doll.___ 1. Well, she's_ the_ girl in the
2. *See additional lyrics*

red____ blue__ jeans, ah, she's the queen__ of ____ all ____ the ____ teens.

Ah, she's the wom - an ____ that I ____ know,__ ah, she's the wom - an that

Chorus

loves ____ me so, say.____ Be - Bop - a - Lu - la, she's my ____ ba - by.

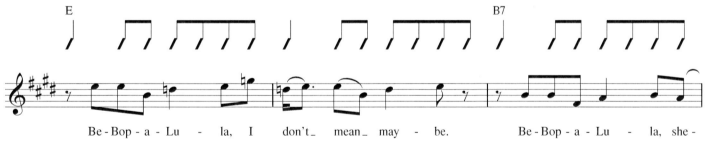

Be - Bop - a - Lu - la, I don't__ mean__ may - be. Be - Bop - a - Lu - la, she -

- e - 's ____ my ba - by doll, my ba - by doll,__ my ba - by doll,__ let's rock.

Guitar Solo

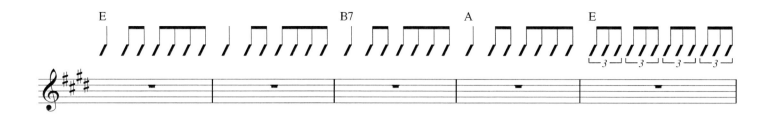

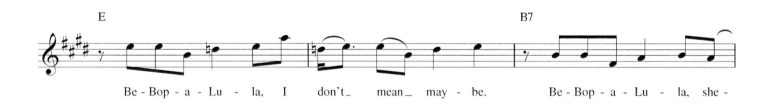

Additional Lyrics

2. Well, now she's the woman that's got that beat,
   Oh, she's the woman with the flyin' feet.
   Ah, she's the woman that walks around the store,
   She's the woman that yells more, more, more, more.

Get Back

Words and Music by John Lennon and Paul McCartney

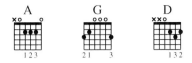

Intro
Moderate Rock

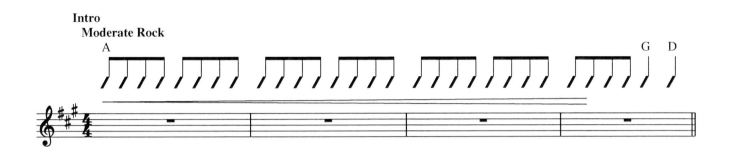

Verse

1. Jo - Jo was a man who thought he was a lon-er, but he knew it could-n't last. Jo -
2. Sweet Lor-et-ta Mar - tin thought she was a wom-an, but she was an-oth-er man. All

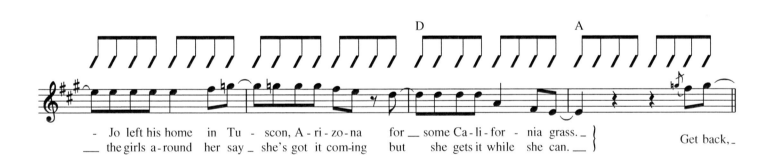

- Jo left his home in Tu - scon, A - ri - zo - na for some Ca - li - for - nia grass.
the girls a-round her say she's got it com-ing but she gets it while she can.

Get back,

Chorus

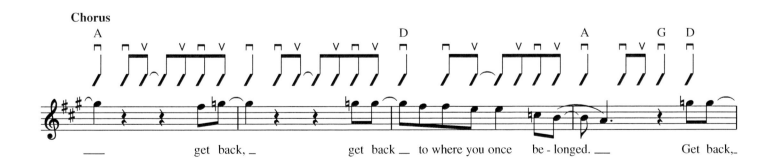

get back, get back to where you once be - longed. Get back,

get back, _ get back _ to where you once be - longed. _ Get back { Jo - Jo. / Lor-et-ta._ }

Guitar Solo

Go home!

Get back, _

Chorus

___ get back, _ back _ to where you once be - longed. _ Get back, _

___ get back, _ back _ to where you once be-longed. _ Here. Uh, get back Jo!

2nd time, D.S. al Coda

Piano Solo

⊕ **Coda**

Guitar Solo

1.

14

C. C. Rider

Adapted and Arranged by Elvis Presley

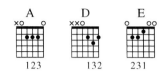

Chorus

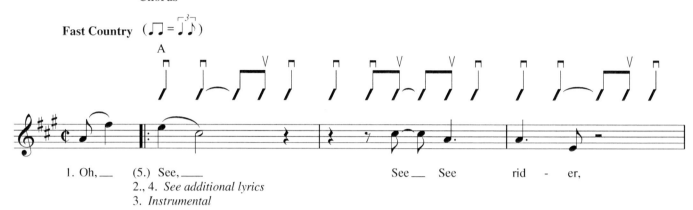

Fast Country

1. Oh, ___ (5.) See, ___
2., 4. *See additional lyrics*
3. *Instrumental*

See ___ See rid - er,

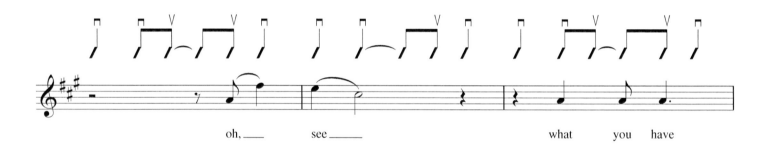

oh, ___ see ___ what you have

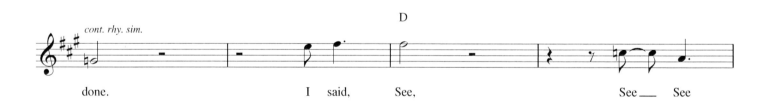

done. I said, See, See ___ See

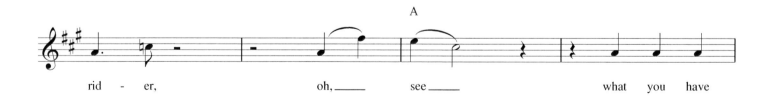

rid - er, oh, ___ see ___ what you have

E

done. ___ Well, you made me ___ love you, ___ and

D   A

now, and now, and now ___ your lov-er man has gone. What'd I say? __

| 1., 2. | 3. | 4. |

5th time, To Coda ⊕   *D.S. al Coda*

___   2. Oh, well, I'm   4. Well, I'm   5. Well, I said,

⊕ **Coda**

Outro

A

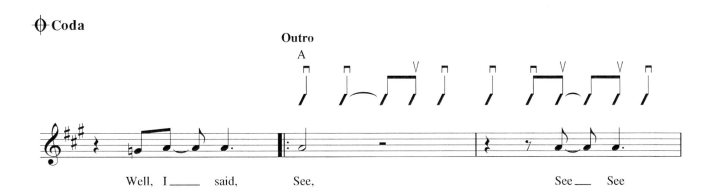

Well, I ___ said,   See,   See ___ See

| 1., 2., 3. | 4. |

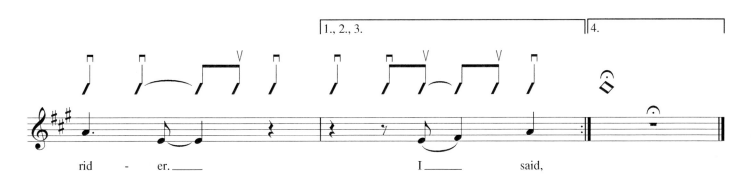

rid - er. ___   I ___   said,

Additional Lyrics

2., 4. { Oh, well, I'm } going away baby
    { Well, I'm }
And I won't be back 'til Fall.
Well, I'm going, going, going, going away, baby,
And I won't be back 'til Fall.
If I find me a good girl,
I won't, I won't, I won't a be back at all.
What'd I say, now.

Chantilly Lace

Words and Music by J.P. Richardson

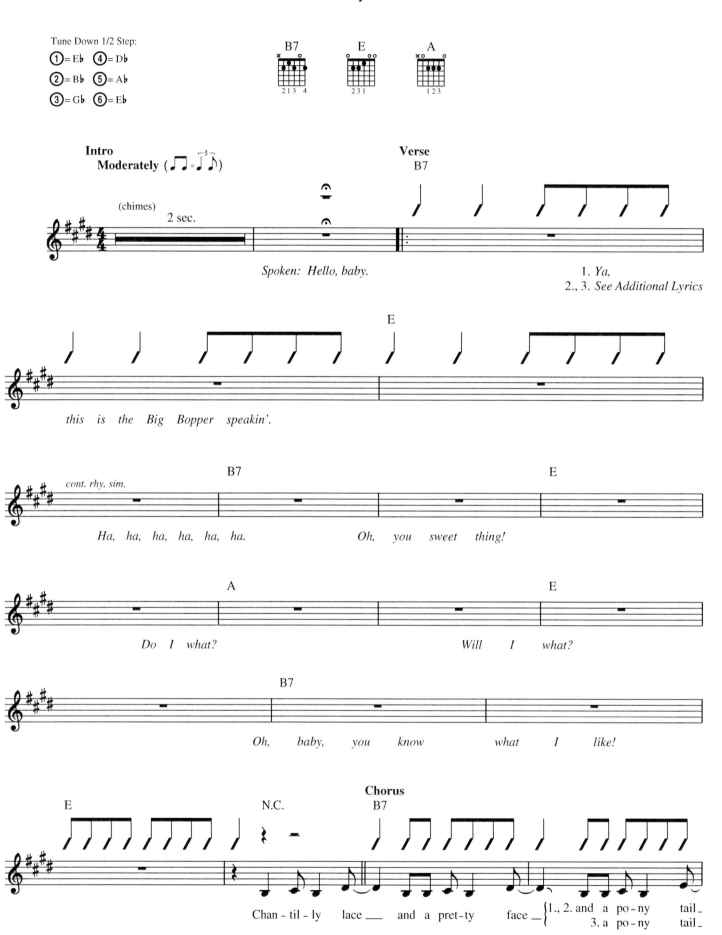

a-hang-in' down, ___ a wig-gle in her walk and a gig-gle in her

1. talk,
2., 3. talk, Lord.

1., 3. Make the world go 'round. ___ 1. There ain't
2. Make the world go 'round, ___ round, round. 2., 3. There ain't a-

noth-in' in the world
noth-in' in the world } like a big eyed girl ___ to make me act so fun-ny, make me

spend my mon-ey, make me feel real loose like a long-necked goose, a-like a

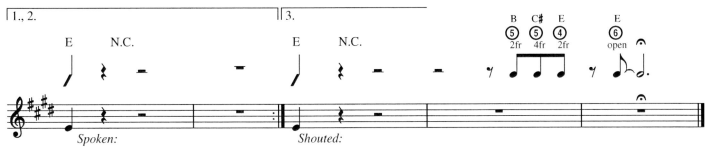

1., 2.
E   N.C.

3.
E   N.C.

B   C#   E   E

girl. *Oh, baby, that's-a what I like!* girl.   *Oh, baby, that's-a what I like!*

Spoken: *Shouted:*

Additional Lyrics

2. *Spoken: What's that baby?*
   But, but, but,
   Oh, honey,
   But, oh baby, you know what I like!

3. *Spoken: What's that honey?*
   Pick you up at eight, and don't be late?
   But, baby, I ain't got no money, honey!
   Ha, ha, ha, ha, ha.
   Oh, alright, honey, you know what I like!

Donna

Words and Music by Ritchie Valens

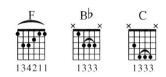

Intro
Moderate ballad

Oh _____ Don - na, oh Don - na.

Oh _____ Don - na, oh Don - na.

Verse

cont. rhy. sim.

1., 3. I had a girl, _____ Don - na _____ was her name.

Since she left me, _____ I've nev - er _____ been the same 'cause I

love _____ my _____ girl. _____ Don - na, _____ where can you

be, _____ where _____ can _____ you be?

To Coda

Verse

2. Now _ that you're gone, _____ I'm left _____ all _____ a - lone.

409

Words and Music by Brian Wilson, Gary Usher and Mike Love

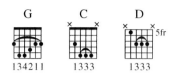

Intro
Moderately

She's real fine, my 4 0 9. ___ She's real fine, my

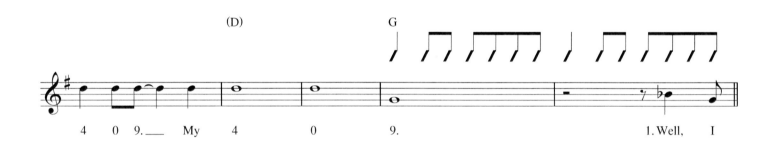

4 0 9. ___ My 4 0 9. 1. Well, I

Verse

saved my pen - nies, and I saved my dimes. ___ (Gid - dy - up, gid - dy - up
2. *See additional lyrics*

4 0 9.) ___ For I knew there would be a time. ___

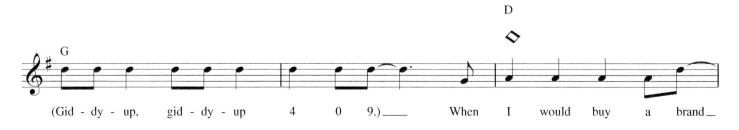

(Gid - dy - up, gid - dy - up 4 0 9.) ___ When I would buy a brand ___

Chorus

cont. rhy. sim.

new   4   0   9.
(4   0   9.)____   4   0   9.)____

Gid - dy - up,   gid - dy - up,   gid - dy - up   4   0   9.   Gid -
(4   0   9.____   4   0   9.)____   Gid - dy - up,   gid - dy - up

- dy - up   4   0   9.   Gid - dy - up   4   0
4   0   9.   4   0   9.____   4   0   9.____

9.   Gid - dy - up   4   0...
Gid - dy - up,   gid - dy   up   4   0   9.)_____

Noth - ing   can   catch   her,   noth - ing   can   touch   my   4   0   9.____

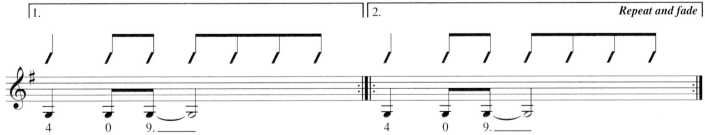

|1.   ‖2.   _**Repeat and fade**_

4   0   9.____   4   0   9.____

Additional Lyrics

2. When I take her to the drag, she really shines.
   (Giddy-up, giddy-up 409.)
   She always turns in the fastest time.
   (Giddy-up, giddy-up 409.)
   My four-speed, dual-quad, posi-traction 409.
   (409. 409.)

Gloria

Words and Music by Van Morrison

Additional Lyrics

2. She comes around here, just about midnight.
   She make me feel so good, Lord, I wanna say she make me feel alright.
   She comes walkin' down my street; a-well, she comes to my house.
   She knock upon my door, and then she comes to my room.
   Then she make me feel alright.

Hang on Sloopy

Words and Music by Wes Farrell and Bert Russell

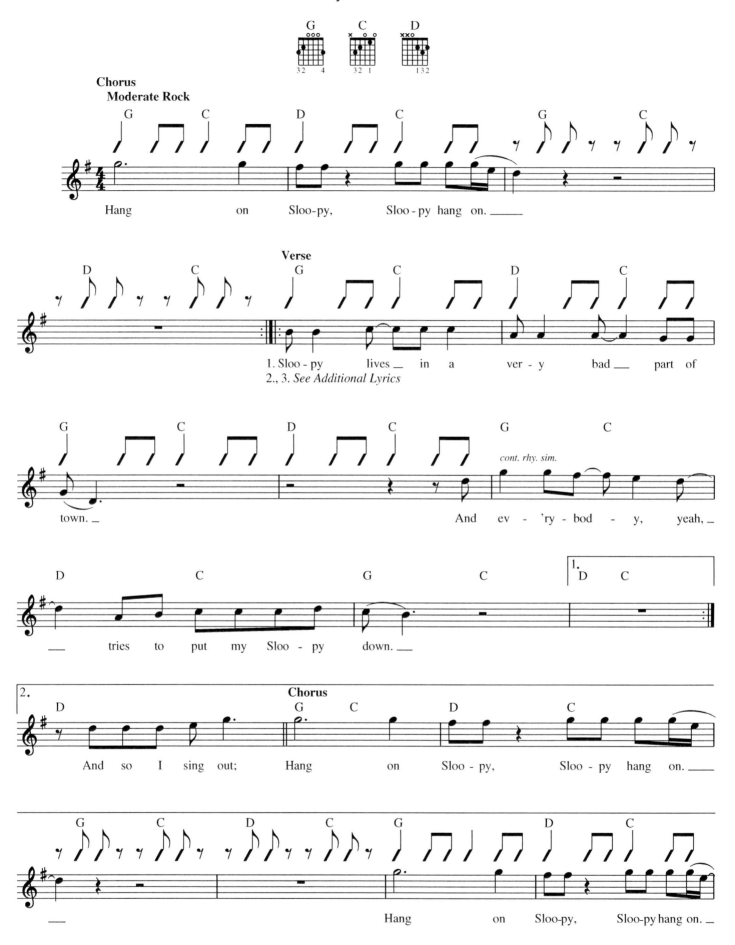

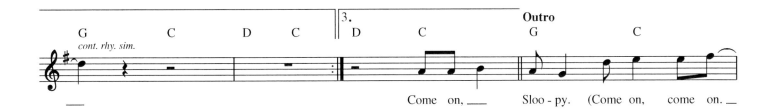

Additional Lyrics

2. Sloopy, I don't care what your daddy do,
   'Cause you know, sloopy girl, I'm in love with you.

3. Sloopy let your hair down, let it hang down on me.
   Sloopy let your hair down, girl, let it hang down on me.

Hanky Panky

Words and Music by Jeff Barry and Ellie Greenwich

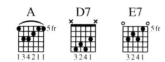

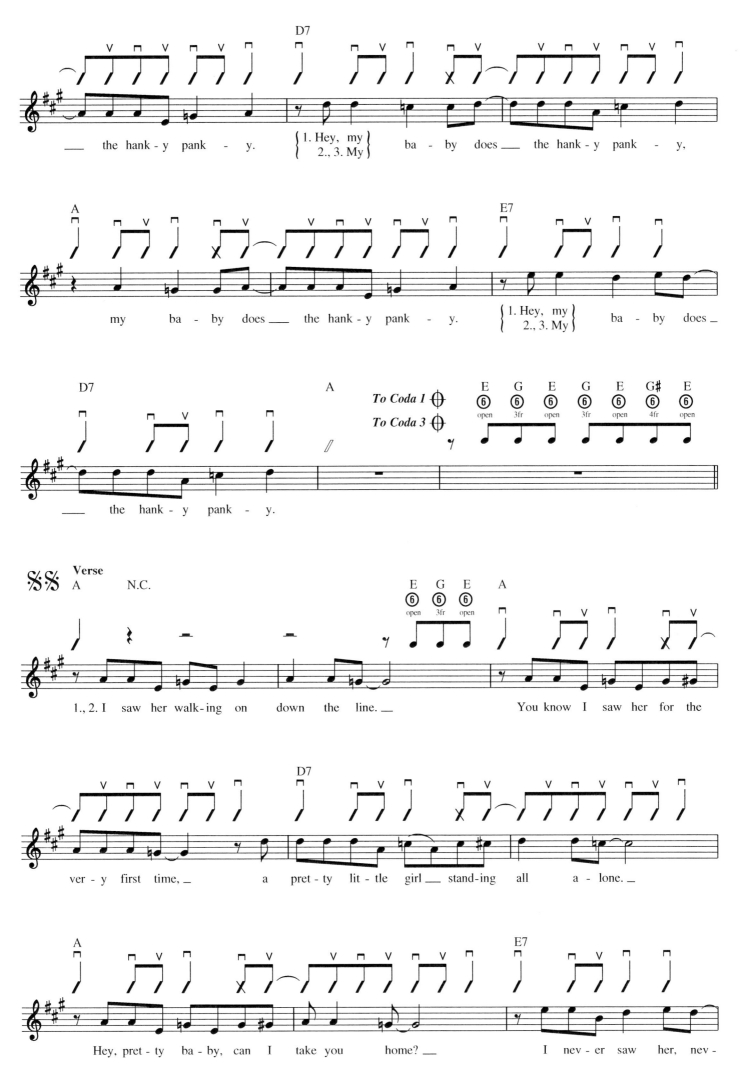

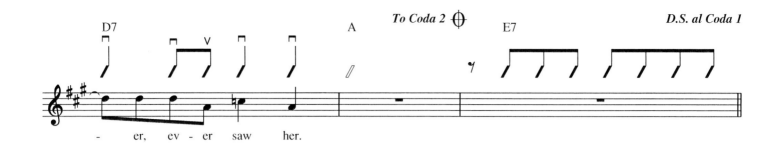

- er, ev - er saw her.

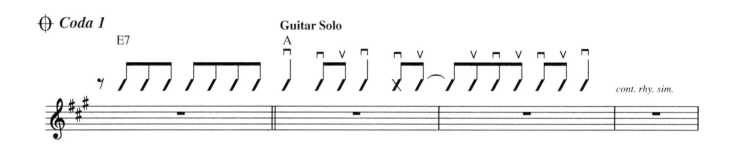

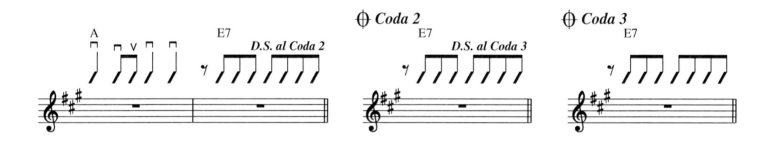

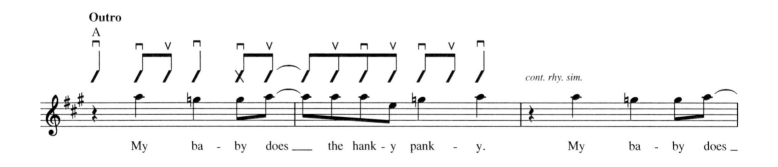

My ba - by does ___ the hank - y pank - y. My ba - by does ___

___ the hank - y pank - y. Yeah, my ba - by does ___ the hank - y pank - y.

Mellow Yellow

Words and Music by Donovan Leitch

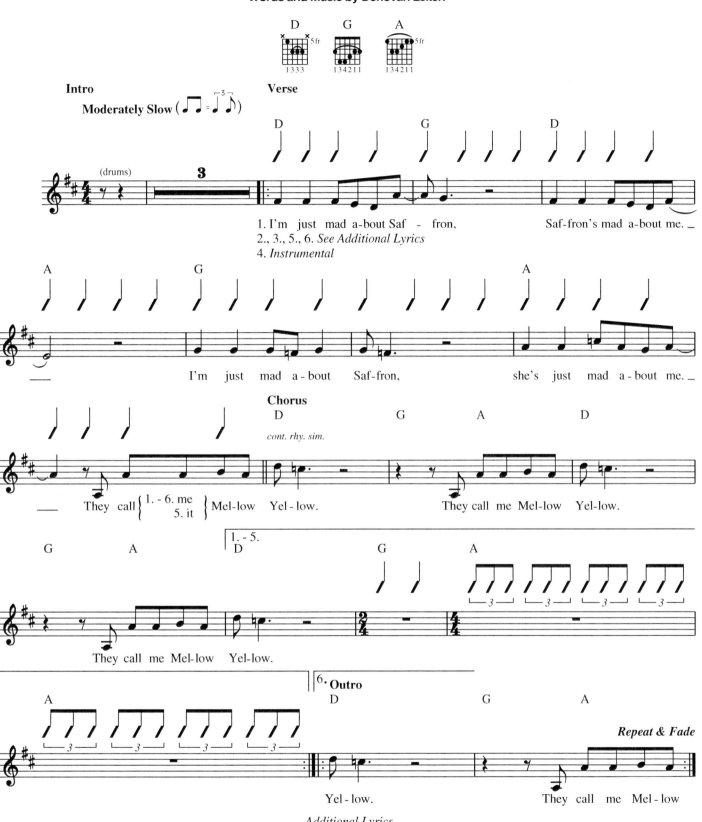

1. I'm just mad a-bout Saf - fron, Saf-fron's mad a-bout me.
2., 3., 5., 6. *See Additional Lyrics*
4. *Instrumental*

I'm just mad a-bout Saf-fron, she's just mad a-bout me.

They call { 1. - 6. me / 5. it } Mel-low Yel-low. They call me Mel-low Yel-low.

They call me Mel-low Yel-low.

Yel - low.

They call me Mel-low

Additional Lyrics

2. I'm just mad about Fourteen,
   Fourteen's mad about me.
   I'm just mad about Fourteen,
   She's just mad about me.

3. Born high, forever to fly,
   Wind velocity: nil.
   Born high, forever to fly,
   If you want your cup I will fill.

5. Electrical banana
   Is going to be a sudden craze.
   Electrical banana
   Is bound to be the very next phase.

6. I'm just mad about Saffron;
   I'm just mad about her.
   I'm just mad about Saffron;
   She's just mad about me.

Hound Dog

Words and Music by Jerry Leiber and Mike Stoller

I Fought the Law

Words and Music by Sonny Curtis

Additional Lyrics

2., 4. I miss my baby and the good fun.
I fought the law and the law won.
I fought the law and the law won.

3. Robbin' people with a six gun.
I fought the law and the law won.
I fought the law and the law won.

Kansas City

Words and Music by Jerry Leiber and Mike Stoller

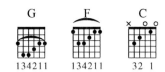

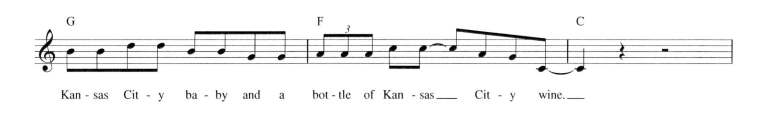

G   F   C

Kan - sas Cit - y ba - by and a bot - tle of Kan - sas___ Cit - y wine.___

Bridge

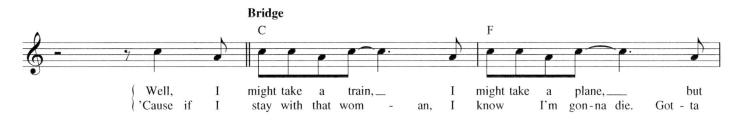

C   F

{ Well, I might take a train,___ I might take a plane,___ but
{ 'Cause if I stay with that wom - an, I know I'm gon-na die. Got - ta

C

if I have to walk I'm goin' just the same___ I'm go - in' to }
find a brand new ba - by and that's the rea - son why I'm go - in' to }

F   C

Kan - sas Cit - y, Kan - sas Cit - y here I come. They got a

G   F   C

cra - zy way of lov - in' there and I'm gon - na get me some.___

1.   2.

                           G

2. I'm go - in' to   They got a cra - zy way of lov - in' there and

F   C

I'm gon - na get me some.___

Additional Lyrics

2. I'm goin' to pack my clothes, leave at the crack of dawn.
   I'm goin' to pack my clothes, leave at the crack of dawn.
   My old lady will be sleepin' and she won't know where I've gone.

La Bamba

By Ritchie Valens

ne - ro, soy cap - i - tan, __ soy cap - i - tan, __ soy cap - i - tan. __

Chorus

Bam - ba, bam - ba. Bam - ba, bam - ba.

Bam - ba, bam - ba. Bam - ba. __ 2. Pa - ra bai - lar La Bam -

Verse

cont. rhy. sim.

- ba. Pa - ra bai - lar La Bam - ba, se ne - ce - si - ta un po - ca de

gra - cia. Un - a po - ca de gra - cia pa'ra mi pa'ra ti ____ y ar - ri - ba, ar - ri -

Guitar solo

Play 7 times

- ba.

Coda

D.S. al Coda

3. Pa - ra bai - lar La Bam - re, por ti se re. ____

Outro-Chorus

Repeat and fade

Bam - ba, bam - ba. Bam - ba, bam - ba.

Mony, Mony

Words and Music by Bobby Bloom, Tommy James, Ritchie Cordell and Bo Gentry

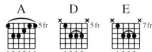

Pre-Chorus

_ (Yeah, _ yeah, _ yeah, _ yeah, yeah. _ yeah,_

𝄋 Chorus

3rd time, w/ Voc. ad lib.

_ Well, you make me feel so _ good._

yeah. Aw!) (Mo-ny, Mo-ny. Mo-ny, Mo-ny.

Yeah, _ { so good. _ Al-right,_

_ al-right. _ Come on, _

Mo-ny, Mo-ny. Mo-ny, Mo-ny. Mo-ny, Mo-ny.

_ come on, _ al-right, _ ba - by. Say yeah,_

_ so good. al-right. _ I say yeah,_

Mo-ny, Mo-ny. Mo-ny, Mo-ny. Mo-ny, Mo-ny.

_ yeah, _ yeah, _ yeah. _ yeah,_

(Yeah, _ yeah, _ yeah, yeah,

2. Wake me, shake me, Mony, Mony.
   Shotgun, get it done. Come on, Mony.
   Don't 'cha stop cookin', it feels so good, yeah.
   Hey! Well, but don't stop now, hey,
   Come on Mony. Well, come on, Mony.

Rock This Town

Words and Music by Brian Setzer

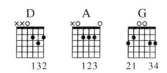

𝄋 **Verse**

Moderately fast

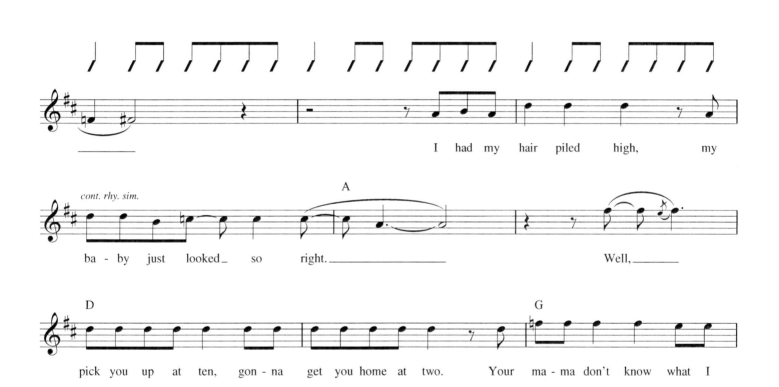

1. Well, my ba - by and me ___ went out ___ late Sat - ur - day night. ___
2., 3. *See additional lyrics*

___ I had my hair piled high, my

cont. rhy. sim.

ba - by just looked ___ so right. ___ Well, ___

pick you up at ten, gon - na get you home at two. Your ma - ma don't know what I

got in store for you. But, ba - by, that's all right, ___ we're look - in' as cool as can be. ___

1.

2. We

Well, let's rock, rock,__ rock,__ rock.__ Rock till we pop, we're gon - na

roll till we drop. We're gon - na rock this town, rock__ it in - side out. __

We're gon - na rock this town, rock__ it in - side out. __

We're gon - na rock this town, rock__ it in - side... Yeah,__ we're gon - na

rock this town,__ tear__ it up,__ we're gon - na rip it down.__ Rock__

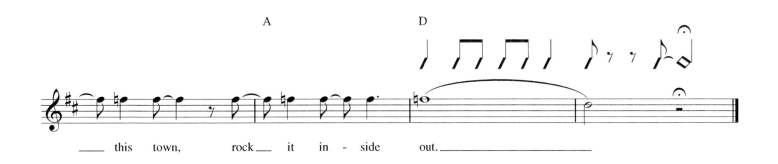

__ this town, rock__ it in - side out._____

Additional Lyrics

2. We found a little place that really didn't look half bad.
   I had a whiskey on the rocks and change of a dollar for the jukebox.
   Well, I put a quarter right into that can,
   But all it played was disco, man.
   Come on, pretty baby, let's get out of here right away.

3. Well, we're havin' a ball just tearing up the big dance floor.
   Well, there's a real square cat; he looks nineteen-seventy-four.
   Well, he looked at me once, he looked at me twice.
   Look at me again and there's gonna be a fight.
   We're gonna rock this town, rip this place apart.

Not Fade Away

Words and Music by Charles Hardin and Norman Petty

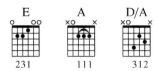

1. I wan-na tell ya how it's gon-na be.
2., 3. *See additional lyrics*

Uh, you're gon-na give your love to me.

I'm gon-na love you night and day.

Chorus

Oh, love is love, not fade a-way.

Uh, well, love is love,____ not fade a - way.

2. Uh, Yeah!

Guitar Solo

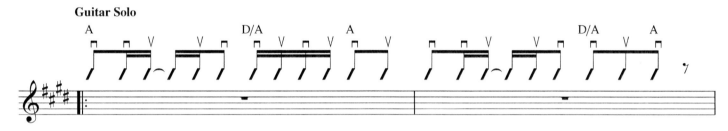

D.S. al Coda

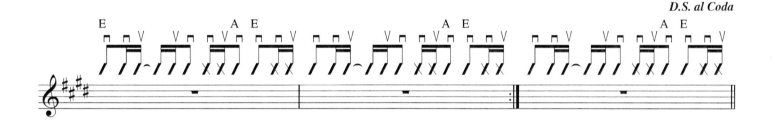

Coda

Outro

w/ Voc. ad lib., till fade

Repeat and fade

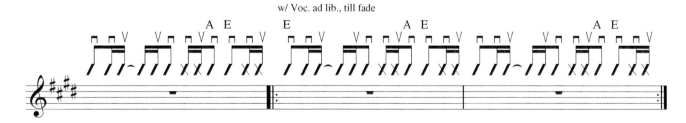

Additional Lyrics

2. Uh, my love's bigger than a Cadillac.
   I try to show it and you drive me back.
   Uh, your love for me has got to be real,
   For you to know just how I feel.

3. I'm gonna tell ya how it's gonna be.
   Uh, you're gonna give your love to me.
   A love that lasts more than one day.

Rain

Words and Music by John Lennon and Paul McCartney

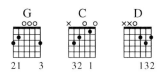

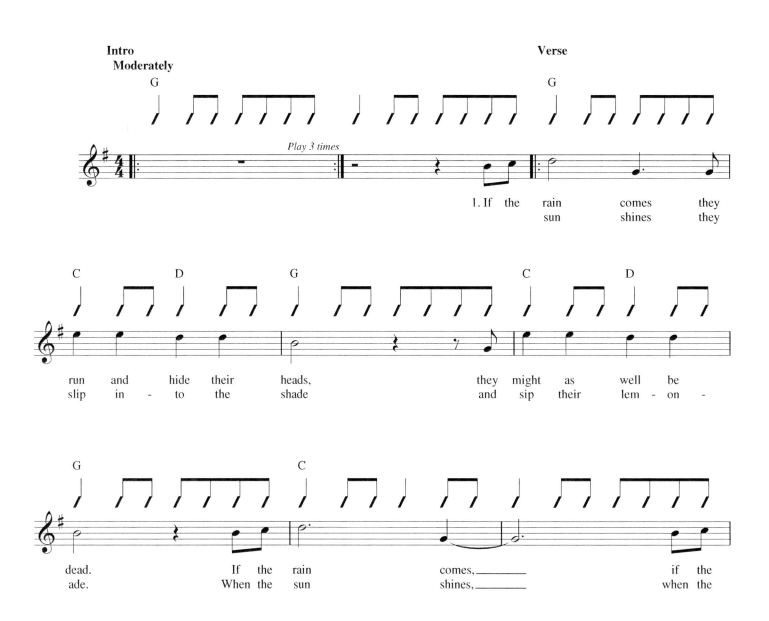

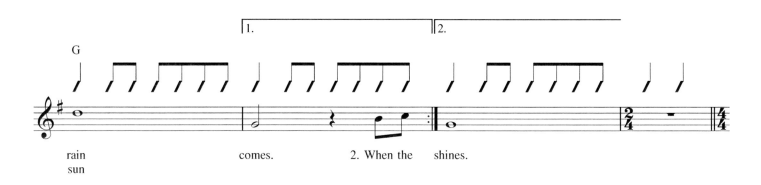

Rock Around the Clock

Words and Music by Max C. Freedman and Jimmy DeKnight

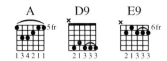

Intro
Moderately fast Rock

N.C.

A

One, two, three o'-clock, four o'-clock rock. Five, six, sev-en o'-clock,

eight o'-clock rock. Nine, ten, e-lev-en o'-clock twelve o'-clock rock. We're gon-na

E9

Verse

A

rock a-round the clock to-night. 1. Put your glad rags on,
2., 4., 5., 6. *See Additional Lyrics*
3. *Instrumental*

cont. rhy. sim.

join me, hon. We'll have some fun when the clock strikes one. We're gon-na

D9

A

rock a-round the clock to-night. We're gon-na rock, rock, rock till

To Coda

E9

A

broad day-light. We're gon-na rock, gon-na rock a-round the clock to-night.

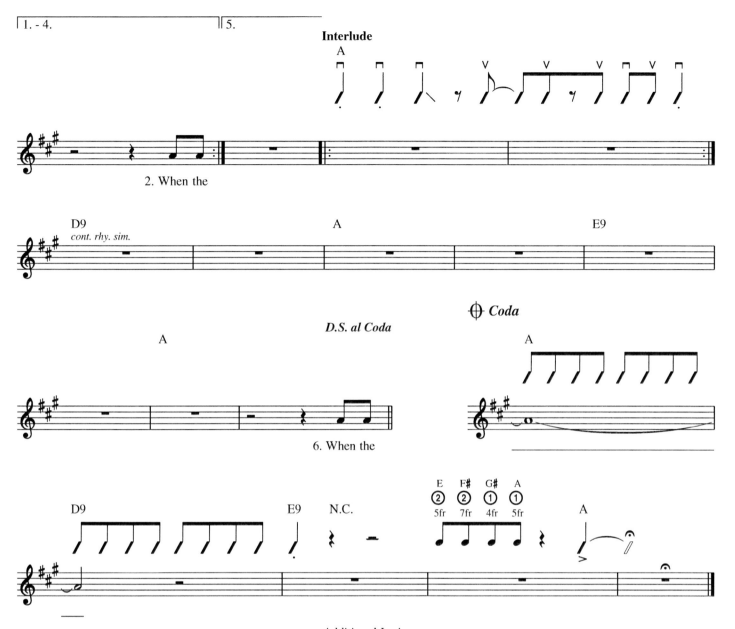

Additional Lyrics

2. When the clock strikes two, three and four,
   If the band slows down we'll yell for more.
   We're gonna rock around the clock tonight.
   We're gonna rock, rock, rock till broad daylight.
   We're gonna rock, gonna rock around the clock tonight.

4. When the chimes ring five, six and seven,
   We'll be right in seventh heaven.
   We're gonna rock around the clock tonight.
   We're gonna rock, rock, rock till broad daylight.
   We're gonna rock, gonna rock around the clock tonight.

5. When it's eight, nine, ten, eleven too,
   I'll be goin' strong and so will you.
   We're gonna rock around the clock tonight.
   We're gonna rock, rock, rock till broad daylight.
   We're gonna rock, gonna rock around the clock tonight.

6. When the clock strikes twelve, we'll cool off then,
   Start a-rockin' 'round the clock again.
   We're gonna rock around the clock tonight.
   We're gonna rock, rock, rock till broad daylight.
   We're gonna rock, gonna rock around the clock tonight.

Rockin' Robin

Words and Music by J. Thomas

Blow, rock - in' rob - in 'cause we're real - ly gon - na rock to - night.

1. *To Coda*

2.

A

Bridge

pret - ty lit - tle ra - ven at the bird band - stand taught

him how to do the bop and it was grand. They

start - ed go - in' stead - y and bless my soul, he

D.S. al Coda

out - bopped the buz - zard and the or - i - ole. 3. He

Coda **Outro**

N.C. *Play 3 times*

Twee - dle - e dee - dle - e - dee, twee - dle - e dee - dle - e - dee. Tweet, tweet.

Additional Lyrics

2. Ev'ry little swallow, ev'ry chickadee,
Ev'ry little bird in the tall oak tree.
The wise old owl, the big black crow,
Flap their wings singin' go, bird, go.

See You Later, Alligator

Words and Music by Robert Guidry

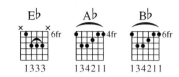

Moderately (♪♪ = ♪³♪)

Verse

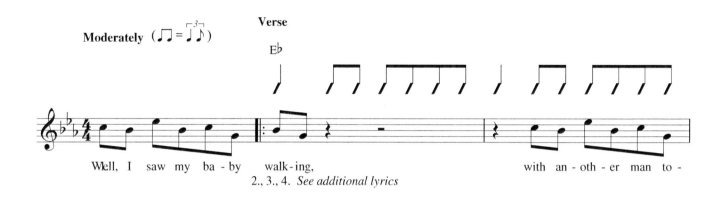

Well, I saw my ba-by walk-ing,

2., 3., 4. See additional lyrics

with an-oth-er man to-

day. __

Well, I saw my ba-by walk-ing,

cont. rhy. sim.

with an-oth-er man to-day. __

When I asked her what's the

mat-ter,

this is what I heard her say.

Chorus

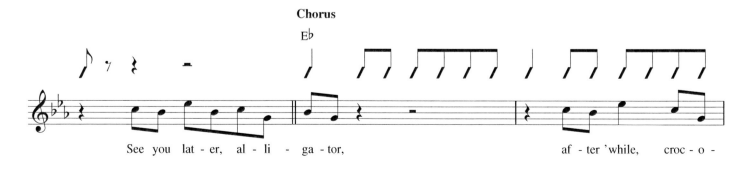

See you lat-er, al-li-ga-tor,

af-ter 'while, croc-o-

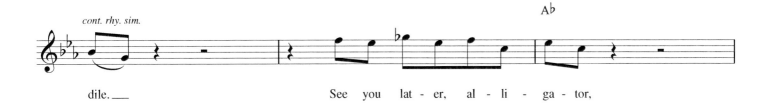

dile. ___   See you lat - er, al - li - ga - tor,

af - ter 'while, croc - o - dile. ___   Can't you see you're in my

way, now,   don't you know you cramp my style?

2. When I thought of what she style?

Additional Lyrics

2. When I thought of what she told me,
   Nearly made me lose my head.
   When I thought of what she told me,
   Nearly made me lose my head.
   But the next time that I saw her,
   Reminded her of what she said.

3. She said, I'm sorry, pretty daddy,
   You know my love is just for you.
   She said, I'm sorry, pretty daddy,
   You know my love is just for you.
   Won't you say that you'll forgive me,
   And say your love for me is true.

4. I said, wait a minute, 'gator,
   I know you meant it just for play.
   I said, wait a minute, 'gator,
   I know you meant it just for play.
   Don't you know you really hurt me,
   And this is what I have to say.

Shake, Rattle and Roll

Words and Music by Charles Calhoun

1. Get

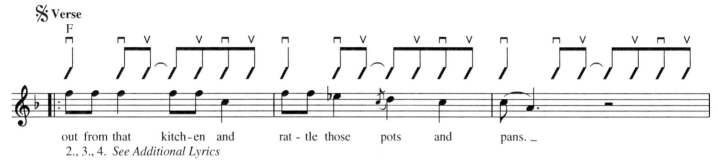

out from that kitch-en and rat-tle those pots and pans. _
2., 3., 4. *See Additional Lyrics*

Get out from that kit-chen and rat-tle those pots and pans. _

Well, roll my break-fast, 'cause I'm a hun - gry __ man. _

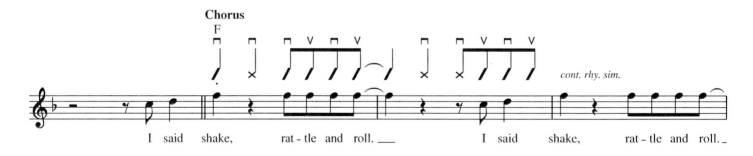

I said shake, rat-tle and roll. __ I said shake, rat-tle and roll. __

__ I said shake, rat-tle and roll. __ I said shake, rat-tle and roll. __

Additional Lyrics

2. Wearin' those dresses, your hair done up so nice.
Wearin' those dresses, your hair done up so nice.
You look so warm, but your heart is cold as ice.

3. I'm like a one-eyed cat, peepin' in a seafood store.
I'm like a one-eyed cat, peepin' in a seafood store.
I can look at you, tell you don't love me no more.

4. I believe you're doin' me wrong and now I know.
I believe you're doin' me wrong and now I know.
The more I work, the faster my money goes.

Stir It Up

Words and Music by Bob Marley

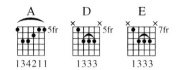

A   D   E

134211   1333   1333

Intro
Moderate Reggae

Chorus

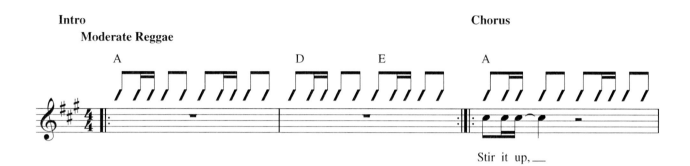

Stir it up, —

lit - tle dar - ling,   stir it up. —   Come on and

stir it up, —   lit - tle dar - ling,   stir it up. —

𝄋 Verse

1. It's been   a long, long time — since I've got you on
2., 3. *See additional lyrics*

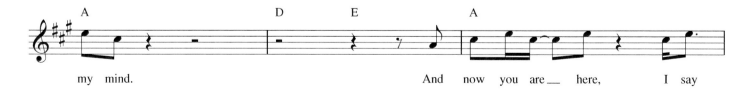

my mind.   And now you are — here,   I say

it's so clear.___ See what we can do, hon - ey, just me and you. Come on and

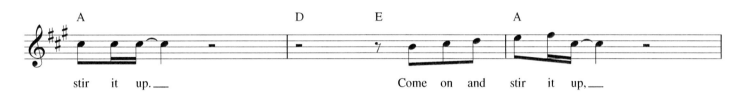

is keep it in. {And/So} stir it up, ___ lit - tle dar - ling,

stir it up. ___ Come on and stir it up, ___

To Coda ⊕

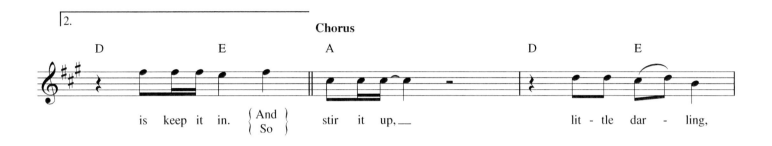

ooh, lit - tle dar - ling, stir it up, ___ yeah.

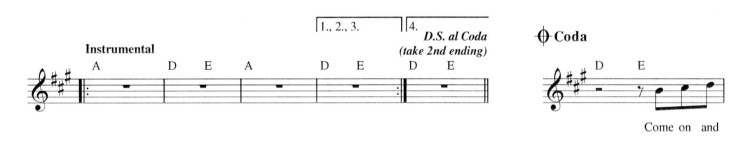

stir it up, oh, lit - tle dar - ling, stir it up. ___

Additional Lyrics

2. I'll push the wood, I'll blaze your fire,
   Then I'll satisfy your, your heart's desire.
   Said I'll stir it, yeah, ev'ry minute, yeah.
   All you got to do, honey, is keep it in.

3. Oh, will you quench me while I'm thirsty?
   Or would you cool me down when I'm hot?
   Your recipe, darling, is so tasty,
   And you sure can stir your pot.

The Twist

Words and Music by Hank Ballard

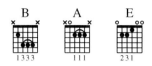

Additional Lyrics

2. My daddy is sleepin' and mama ain't around.
   Yeah, daddy's just sleepin' and mama ain't around.
   We're gonna twist, a-twist, a-twistin',
   Till we tear the house down.

3. Yeah, you should see my little sis.
   You should see my, my little sis.
   She really knows how to rock,
   She knows how to twist.

When Will I Be Loved

Words and Music by Phil Everly

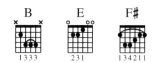

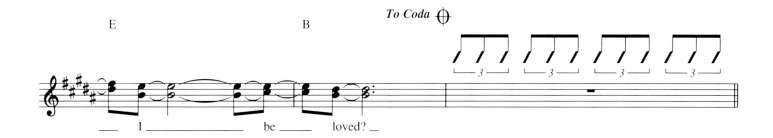

_I _ be _ loved? _

Bridge

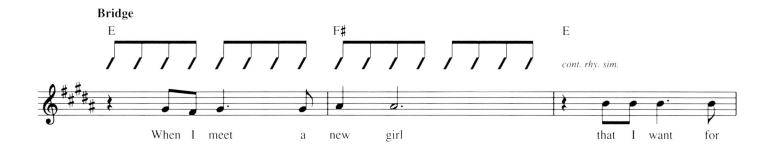

When I meet a new girl

that I want for

mine, _ she al - ways _ breaks my heart in two. _ It hap - pens _ ev - 'ry

1.

time.

2.

D.S. al Coda

time.

Coda

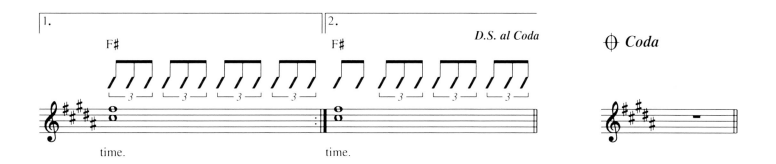

Outro

Repeat & Fade

When will I _ be _ loved? _

Additional Lyrics

3., 4. I've been cheated,
Been mistreated.
When will I be loved?

STRUM IT GUITAR LEGEND

Strum It is the series designed especially to get you playing (and singing!) along with your favorite songs. The idea is simple – the songs are arranged using their original keys in lead sheet format, providing you with the authentic chords for each song, beginning to end. Rhythm slashes are written above the staff. Strum the chords in the rhythm indicated. Use the chord diagrams found at the top of the first page of the arrangement for the appropriate chord voicings. The melody and lyrics are also shown to help you keep your spot and sing along.

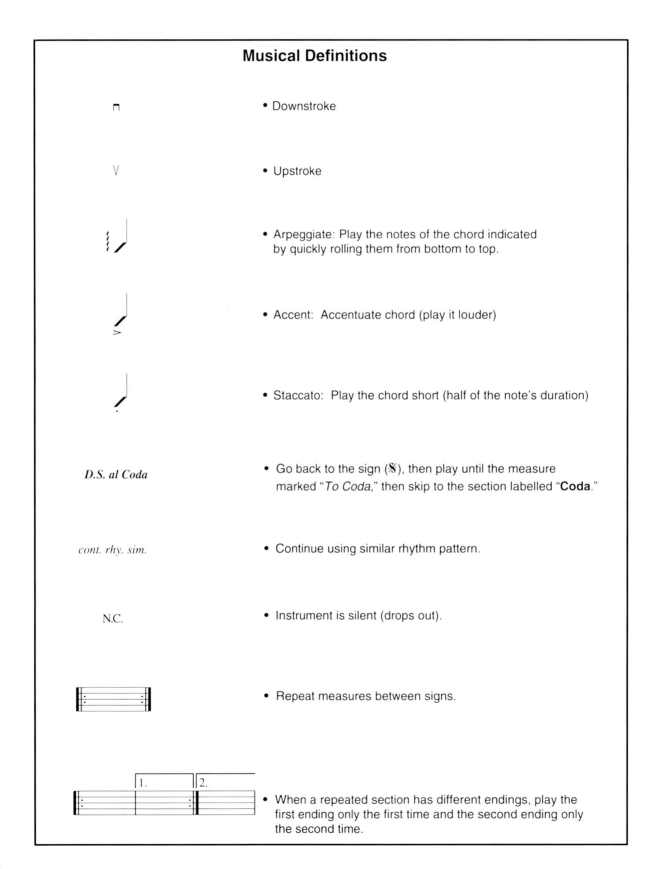

Musical Definitions

⊓
- Downstroke

V
- Upstroke

- Arpeggiate: Play the notes of the chord indicated by quickly rolling them from bottom to top.

- Accent: Accentuate chord (play it louder)

- Staccato: Play the chord short (half of the note's duration)

D.S. al Coda
- Go back to the sign (𝄋), then play until the measure marked "*To Coda*," then skip to the section labelled "**Coda**."

cont. rhy. sim.
- Continue using similar rhythm pattern.

N.C.
- Instrument is silent (drops out).

- Repeat measures between signs.

|1. |2.
- When a repeated section has different endings, play the first ending only the first time and the second ending only the second time.